International Cooking Collection

Food Processor Cooking

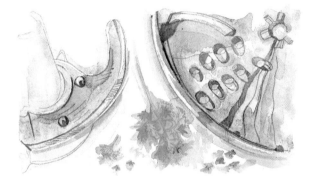

International Cooking Collection

Food Processor Cooking

Carol Bowen

CONTENTS

Published exclusively for Cupress (Canada) Ltd
20 Torbay Road, Markham, Ontario L3R 1G6 Canada
by Woodhead-Faulkner (Publishers) Ltd, Simon & Schuster International Group

This edition first published 1988
© Woodhead-Faulkner (Publishers) Ltd 1988
ISBN 0-920691-80-3
Printed and bound in Italy

INTRODUCTION

If you're the sort of cook who hesitates to try a recipe because it calls for a finely chopped ingredient, a food to be pureed, sieved or grated finely, then you will have warmly welcomed the recent arrival of the food processor, which will easily and speedily dispense with those arduous and muscle-aching food preparation chores, opening new doors to delicious meals.

However, with availability has also come variety—and the decision of which processor to buy has become more complex. Size, features, price and performance are just some of the important considerations. Every food processor will mix, grind, slice, shred, blend, knead, grate, puree and chop at the very minimum using the standard metal chopping blade, grating disc and slicing disc attachments provided; many, with optional extras, will do a lot more.

BASIC FOOD PROCESSOR MODELS
There are two basic types of food processor, categorized by the motors they use. Most are powered by a belt-drive motor, with the bowl placed beside the motor. More expensive but more durable is the direct drive motor processor where the bowl usually sits on top of the motor.

Every manufacturer provides the three basic attachments, plus a spatula and feed tube. In addition, the following may also be available:
● plastic blending blade (often a standard too) for mixing doughs, batters, creamed cake mixtures and sauces
● whipping blade (increasingly becoming a standard attachment) for whipping cream, whipping egg whites and making light-as-air sponge cakes
● French fry or chipper disc
● juice extractor or citrus press
● soft ice cream maker
● dough kit
● Parmesan cheese grater disc
● ripple-cut disc

Some models also offer a wider selection of the basic attachments: fine, medium or coarse grater; thin or thick slicer; and even a special coleslaw grater disc. Use different discs, if you have them, to provide a variety of shapes and textures—particularly important in salads and vegetable dishes. Many manufacturers will take separate orders for an additional bowl—a very useful extra that helps cut down on annoying mid-recipe bowl rinsing.

Many processors simply work on one speed, but with some the speed can be increased by turning a dial or pressing a button. A pulse button—where action can be added at the touch of a finger—is a good feature to look out for, as it gives very precise control when processing small quantities or delicate items.

With the trend toward co-ordinated kitchens, food processors now come in a variety of colors and, if you're planning a new kitchen, one model can be built into a worktop for convenience.

EFFICIENT USE

Having chosen the best processor for your requirements, the next considera-
tion is how to use it most efficiently. Processors are the new 'merlins' of the
kitchen, but their wizardry can go haywire if you don't observe a few basic
rules, which I call the 'three Rs':

Right Order: There is a logical order to processing foods. It comes quickly and
naturally with use but as a general guide:
- process foods that require a dry bowl first, then remove
- secondly, slice or grate any foods that need to be incorporated into chopped
mixtures later; remove
- next process foods that require a long chopping time
- follow with delicate foods that require short chopping times to give an
overall uniform mixture
- finally blend or mix any items together

Right Time: Speed is one of the major features of the food processor but
timings are critical. Follow the recipe guidelines exactly or err on the side of
safety by under-processing, adding extra action via the pulse button if your
model has one. It's only too easy to end up with a vegetable puree instead of
chopped vegetables if you don't keep an eye on what's happening.

Right Load: Processing more than the ideal load for your processor will not
save time but simply strain the motor and give uneven results. It is easier and
safer to process in batches. Ideal load capacities for the standard model used in
this book are:
- 2 lb bread dough—to make and knead
- 2½ cups cooked vegetables and stock—to puree for soup
- 1 lb meat—for chopping or grinding
- 4-egg Victoria sandwich cake—to mix
- 1¼ lb shortcrust pastry—to mix
- 2½ cups mayonnaise—to make

SAFETY AND CARE

Never immerse the motor base in water—simply wipe with a damp cloth.
Never leave blades and discs to soak in water for unsuspecting hands.
Never use fingers, spoons or other implements instead of the special pusher
provided for use with the feed tube.
Make sure that the bowl is safely locked into position before fitting attachments
and before switching on.
Don't attempt to touch the food before the blade has stopped; a safety lock will
ensure that the motor stops when the lid is opened, but the blade takes a little
longer to stop unless you have a model with a blade brake.

PROCESSOR SHORT-CUT TIPS

- Make speedy long-lasting garlic puree in bulk. Fit the metal chopping blade.
Place about 20 cloves garlic in the processor bowl with a pinch of salt and
process for about 20 seconds, until smooth, scraping down once. Add 2
tablespoons oil and process for 5 seconds. Place in a screw-topped jar and
cover with a little oil. Store in the refrigerator for up to 2 months. Use ½–1
teaspoon puree for each garlic clove required.

- Make fresh breadcrumbs speedily. Fit the metal chopping blade, then, with the motor running, add bread cubes through the feed tube and process for 5–8 seconds.
- Chop herbs for use in salads, savory dishes and garnishing. Fit the metal chopping blade. Place the herbs in the processor bowl or, with the motor running, add through the feed tube. Process for 3–6 seconds, chop to desired fineness. Bag and freeze if you wish.
- Save time on grating cheese. Grate or slice in the processor and freeze in plastic bags for instant use in sauces, toppings, etc.
- Slice halved or quartered citrus fruits in bulk. Freeze and use for drinks and garnishes.
- Make chocolate decorations for cakes and desserts, using the grating disc. Chocolate at room temperature will give curls; hard chocolate will give chips.
- Chop nuts speedily: fit the metal chopping blade and process for 2–5 seconds to desired fineness.

RECIPE GUIDELINES

All the recipes and timings given in this book refer to a standard 1 quart food processor model with just the three basic attachments—metal chopping blade, medium slicing disc and grating disc; notes are given for use of optional extras where applicable.

It is important to note that, before adding directly to the processor bowl, carrots, celery, zucchini and bananas should be cut into 2 or 3 large pieces, depending on their size; cucumbers, peppers and onions, except small ones, should be quartered; meat should be cut roughly into 2 inch squares. This will aid the chopping or grinding process.

Foods to be sliced or grated should be cut into pieces to fit into the feed tube and pushed down to the disc with the pusher.

Ingredients are introduced in the right order for maximum efficiency and all processing has been timed accurately for the best results.

Only wash the food processor bowl during a recipe it if says so—if it isn't stated, it isn't necessary.

NOTES

All spoon measurements are level.

Use U.S. grade large eggs unless otherwise stated.

Ovens should be preheated to the temperature specified.

Freshly ground black pepper is intended where pepper is listed.

Fresh herbs are used unless otherwise stated. If unobtainable, dried herbs can be substituted in cooked dishes but halve the quantities.

Basic recipes are marked with an asterisk and given on pages 76–9. Increase or decrease the basic quantities in proportion to obtain the amount required.

PATÉS, MOUSSES, SOUPS & DIPS

SMOKED TROUT PATÉ

A delicious creamy paté that freezes so well it is worth making in bulk. Thaw in the refrigerator overnight or at room temperature for 4–6 hours.

*1 lb smoked trout, skinned
    and boned
1/2 cup butter, softened
1 tablespoon lemon juice
1 tablespoon creamed
    horseradish*

*salt and pepper to taste
TO GARNISH:
lemon twists
parsley sprigs*

**Serves 6
Preparation time:**
10 minutes, plus
chilling
Freezing:
Recommended

1. Fit the metal chopping blade. Place the trout and butter in the processor bowl and process for 10–15 seconds, until smooth.
2. Add the lemon juice, horseradish, and salt and pepper and process for about 5 seconds, until smooth and creamy.
3. Spoon into 6 individual dishes and chill until firm.
4. Garnish with lemon twists and parsley and serve with toast or crackers.

CREAMY TARAMASALATA

This popular Greek appetizer is delicious served with crusty bread, pitta bread or toast. It can also be used as a spread for canapés or a dip for vegetable sticks.

*1/4 lb smoked cods' roe,
    skinned
4 slices bread, crusts
    removed and cubed
3 tablespoons lemon juice*

*1 clove garlic
2/3 cup olive oil
TO GARNISH:
black olives
lemon slices*

**Serves 6–8
Preparation time:**
10 minutes
Freezing:
Not recommended

1. Fit the metal chopping blade. Place the cods' roe, bread, lemon juice and garlic in the processor bowl and process for 10–15 seconds, until smooth; scrape down the bowl if necessary halfway through processing.
2. With the motor running, slowly pour the oil through the feed tube, and process for about 1 second, to mix.
3. Spoon into a small serving bowl and garnish with black olives and lemon slices.

TRADITIONAL FARMHOUSE PATÉ

½ lb bacon	*1 clove garlic*
½ lb pork shoulder steak	*½ teaspoon dried*
½ lb pigs' liver	*marjoram*
½ lb pork sausage meat	*salt and pepper to taste*
1 small onion	

Serves 8–10
Preparation time:
20 minutes, plus
chilling
Cooking time:
1½–1¾ hours
Freezing:
Recommended

1. Stretch the bacon with a palette knife and use two-thirds of the rashers to line a 7½ × 3½ × 2½ inch loaf pan.
2. Fit the metal chopping blade. Place the pork in the processor bowl and process for about 5 seconds, until finely chopped.
3. Add the remaining ingredients and process for 6–8 seconds, until finely chopped. Place in the pan, smoothing the top. Cover with the remaining bacon.
4. Cover with foil and place in a roasting pan half-filled with hot water. Cook in a 325°F oven for 1½–1¾ hours, until firm.
5. Replace the foil with waxed paper, place a 2 lb weight on top and leave until cold. Chill overnight.
6. Turn out, slice and serve with toast and salad.

POTTED CHEESE RESERVE

Potted cheese is an old English favorite. Use any variety or a mixture of the great English cheeses such as sharp Cheddar, Stilton, Wensleydale, or any complementary American or European cheeses you like.

8 oz cheese (see above)
6 tablespoons sweet butter,
   softened
1 tablespoon snipped
   chives

2 tablespoons port
pinch of ground red pepper
walnut halves to garnish

1. Fit the grating disc and grate the cheese; remove and set aside.
2. Fit the metal chopping or plastic blending blade. Place the butter, cheese, chives, port and ground red pepper in the processor bowl and process for 3–5 seconds, to blend thoroughly.
3. Spoon into a terrine or 4 small serving dishes, cover and chill for 1 hour.
4. Garnish with walnut halves and serve with crackers, crispbreads or celery.

Serves 4
Preparation time:
10–15 minutes,
plus chilling
Freezing:
Recommended for
up to 1 month

CHICKEN AND BRANDY MOUSSE

One of the easiest mousses to make, yet you'd never believe it by the taste. Garnish with an elegant center-piece, e.g. orange segments or edible nasturtium flowers, tossed with watercress sprigs or shredded radicchio.

2¹/₂ oz package aspic jelly powder	*1 tablespoon tomato paste*
2¹/₂ cups very hot chicken stock	*1 teaspoon chopped parsley*
	2 egg yolks
¹/₂ lb smoked chicken, skinned	*1 cup heavy cream*
	¹/₂ cup brandy
	pepper to taste

Serves 6–8
Preparation time: 15 minutes, plus chilling
Freezing: Recommended

1. Place the aspic in a bowl, gradually add the very hot stock and beat well until dissolved. Leave until cool but not set.
2. Fit the metal chopping blade. Place the cooled aspic and remaining ingredients in the processor bowl and process for about 20 seconds, until smooth and creamy.
3. Spoon into an oiled 5 cup fluted ring mold and chill until set.
4. To serve, dip briefly into hot water, turn out onto a serving dish and fill the center with a salad garnish.

CRAB AND CUCUMBER MOUSSE

This fresh, light mousse makes a stunning cold buffet centerpiece if set in a fish-shaped or fluted ring mold.

¹/₃ lb cucumber	*1 tablespoon tomato catsup*
1 envelope gelatin, soaked in 3 tablespoons water	*dash of Tabasco sauce*
¹/₂ lb crab meat, flaked	*²/₃ cup heavy cream*
¹/₂ cup Mayonnaise*	*salt and pepper to taste*
1 tablespoon lemon juice	*cucumber slices to garnish*

1. Fit the metal chopping blade. Peel the cucumber, place in the processor bowl and process for about 1 second, to chop. Remove and set aside.
2. Heat the gelatin gently until dissolved.
3. Place the crab meat, gelatin, mayonnaise, lemon juice, tomato catsup, Tabasco sauce, and salt and pepper in the processor bowl and process for about 20 seconds, until smooth.
4. Add the cucumber and process for 1 second, to mix.

5. Whip the heavy cream until it stands in soft peaks (using the processor whipping blade if your model has one), then fold into the crab mixture with a metal spoon.

6. Spoon into an oiled 4 cup decorative fish or fluted ring mold and chill until set.

7. To serve, dip briefly into hot water, turn out onto a serving dish and garnish with cucumber.

Serves 6
Preparation time:
30 minutes, plus chilling
Freezing:
Not recommended

THREE DIP CRUDITÉS

Crisp vegetable sticks served with a variety of dips make a delicious stand-up appetizer to serve with drinks.

DEVILED HAM DIP:
1/4 onion
1/4 red pepper
1 slice ham
6 tablespoons Mayonnaise*
2 tablespoons corn relish
1/2 teaspoon mustard
salt and pepper to taste
WATERCRESS AND
* ORANGE DIP:*
1/2 bunch watercress
flesh of 1/2 orange
1/2 cup Mayonnaise*
1 tablespoon orange juice
1 teaspoon finely grated
* orange rind*
salt and pepper to taste

COOL AVOCADO DIP:
1/2 small ripe avocado
2 teaspoons lemon juice
1/2 cup Mayonnaise*
1 tablespoon chopped
* parsley*
salt and pepper to taste
VEGETABLE CRUDITÉS:
4 large carrots
1/4 cucumber
1 red and 1 green or
* yellow pepper, cored*
* and seeded*
TO SERVE:
about 18 olives
about 18 small mushrooms
crisp crackers

Serves 4–6
Preparation time:
20–25 minutes
Freezing:
Not recommended

Deviled Ham Dip
Fit the metal chopping blade. Place the onion, red pepper and ham in the processor bowl and process for 3–4 seconds, until finely chopped. Add the remaining ingredients and process for 1–2 seconds, to blend. Spoon into a small bowl, cover and chill until required.

Watercress and Orange Dip
Fit the metal chopping blade. Place the watercress in the processor bowl and process for 1–2 seconds, until coarsely chopped. Add the remaining ingredients and process for about 2 seconds, until blended. Spoon into a small bowl, cover and chill until required.

Cool Avocado Dip
Fit the metal chopping blade. Place all the ingredients in the processor bowl and process for about 5 seconds, until smooth. Spoon into a bowl, cover and chill until required.

Vegetable Crudités
Fit the slicing disc and slice the vegetables. (Or use a chipper or French fry disc if your processor has one.)

To Serve:
Arrange the crudités on a large plate with the olives, mushrooms and crackers. Serve with the dips.

MUSTARD AND SOUR CREAM DIP

A delicious, creamy yet crunchy, dip to serve with smoked fish as an appetizer.

1 red dessert apple, cored
1 teaspoon lemon juice
4 scallions
1¹/₄ cups sour cream

2–3 teaspoons French
*   mustard*
salt and pepper to taste

1. Fit the grating disc and grate the apple. Place in a mixing bowl. Add the lemon juice and toss well.
2. Fit the metal chopping blade. Place the scallions in the processor bowl and process for 2–3 seconds, until coarsely chopped. Set aside about 2 teaspoons for garnish.
3. Add all the remaining ingredients to the processor bowl and process for 1–2 seconds, to blend.
4. Spoon into a small bowl and sprinkle with the reserved chopped scallion. Cover and chill until required.
5. Serve with smoked mackerel or trout.

Serves 4
Preparation time:
10 minutes
Freezing:
Not recommended

BACON AND SPLIT PEA SOUP

2 oz bacon
1 large onion
2 tablespoons butter
⅔ cup yellow split peas

3 cups light stock
pepper to taste
chopped parsley to garnish

Serves 4
Preparation time:
10 minutes
Cooking time:
1½ hours
Freezing:
Recommended

1. Fit the metal chopping blade. Place the bacon in the processor bowl and process for 3–4 seconds, to chop. Remove and set aside.
2. Add the onion to the processor bowl and process for 2–3 seconds, until finely chopped.
3. Melt the butter in a large heavy-based pan, add the onion and bacon and fry for 5 minutes, until softened.
4. Add the split peas and stock, cover and bring to the boil, then simmer for 1½ hours, stirring occasionally. Cool slightly.
5. Puree the soup in the processor bowl, in batches if necessary, for about 8 seconds per batch.
6. Return to the pan, season with pepper and heat gently.
7. Pour into a warmed tureen, garnish with parsley and serve with crusty bread.

CLASSIC SPANISH GAZPACHO

*3 small slices whole wheat
   bread, cubed*
2¹/₂ cups tomato juice
*1 green and 1 red pepper,
   cored and seeded*
¹/₂ cucumber
1 large onion
*1¹/₂ lb tomatoes, skinned
   and seeded*
2 cloves garlic

¹/₄ cup olive oil
*2 tablespoons red wine
   vinegar*
¹/₂ teaspoon dried basil
salt and pepper to taste
TO SERVE:
croutons
*chopped onion, pepper,
   olives and cucumber*

1. Place the bread in a bowl, pour over the tomato juice and leave for 5 minutes. Remove the bread, squeezing to extract the juice, and set aside. Reserve the tomato juice.
2. Fit the metal chopping blade. Place the bread, peppers, cucumber, onion, tomatoes and garlic in the processor bowl and process, in batches if necessary, for about 20 seconds per batch, until smooth.
3. Add all the remaining ingredients and process, in batches, for 3–5 seconds per batch, to blend. Pour into a tureen and chill for at least 1 hour.
4. Serve with bowls of croutons, and chopped onion, pepper, olives and cucumber, for sprinkling on the soup.

Serves 4–6
Preparation time:
15 minutes, plus chilling
Freezing:
Not recommended

WATERCRESS SOUP

A delicious fresh-looking soup, good served hot or chilled.

2 bunches watercress	*2 cups vegetable stock*
1 onion	*2 cups milk*
2 tablespoons butter	*²⁄₃ cup whipping cream*
1 lb potatoes, chopped	*salt and pepper to taste*

Serves 6
Preparation time:
15 minutes
Cooking time:
40 minutes
Freezing:
Recommended at
end of stage 6

1. Discard the lower stalks from the watercress.
2. Fit the metal chopping blade. Place the watercress in the processor bowl and process for 2–3 seconds, until coarsely chopped. Remove and set aside.
3. Add the onion to the processor bowl and process for 2–3 seconds, until finely chopped.
4. Melt the butter in a pan, add the onion and watercress, cover and cook gently for 5 minutes.
5. Add the potatoes, stock, milk, and salt and pepper, bring to the boil, then cover and simmer for 35 minutes. Cool slightly.
6. Puree the soup in the processor bowl, in batches if necessary, for about 8 seconds per batch.
7. To serve hot, return the soup to the pan, stir in the cream and heat gently. Pour into individual warmed soup bowls.
8. To serve cold, pour into individual soup bowls and chill. Swirl a spoonful of cream on top of each just before serving.

BRANDIED FRENCH ONION SOUP

A classic French onion soup prepared the 'no-tears' way in the processor. The addition of brandy and floating cheese croute garnish makes it a sophisticated soup for serving at a dinner party.

1 lb onions	*5 cups rich beef stock*
¹⁄₄ cup butter	*4 oz Gruyère or Swiss*
1 tablespoon salad oil	*cheese*
¹⁄₂ teaspoon light brown	*4 thick slices French bread*
sugar	*2 teaspoons snipped chives*
2 tablespoons all-purpose	*2 tablespoons brandy*
flour	*salt and pepper to taste*

1. Fit the slicing disc and slice the onions.
2. Heat the butter and oil in a large heavy-based pan, add the onions, cover and cook for 20 minutes.
3. Stir in the sugar, increase the heat and cook for 5–10 minutes, until the onions turn a rich golden color, stirring frequently.
4. Stir in the flour and cook until browned, then gradually add the stock. Season with salt and pepper. Bring to the boil, then cover and simmer for 20 minutes.
5. Meanwhile, fit the grating disc and grate the cheese.
6. Toast the bread on one side, turn and sprinkle with the cheese; broil until bubbling. Sprinkle with the chives.
7. Add the brandy to the soup and reheat gently. Pour into warmed soup bowls and top each with a cheese croute.

Serves 4
Preparation time:
15 minutes
Cooking time:
45–50 minutes
Freezing:
Recommended, without the croutes

PORK WITH ORCHARD STUFFING

2 parsley sprigs
4 slices bread, cubed
1 small onion
1 celery stick
1 cooking apple, peeled,
*   cored and quartered*
⅓ cup cashew nuts
2 tablespoons butter

2 teaspoons lemon juice
4 lb loin of pork, boned
*   and scored*
FOR THE SAUCE:
2 teaspoons cornstarch
½ cup apple juice
1 tablespoon heavy cream
salt and pepper to taste

Serves 6
Preparation time:
15 minutes
Cooking time:
About 2½ hours
Freezing:
Not recommended

1. Fit the metal chopping blade. With the motor running, add the parsley and bread through the feed tube and process for about 5 seconds, to make herby crumbs. Remove and set aside.
2. Place the onion and celery in the processor bowl and process for 3–4 seconds, to chop. Remove and set aside.
3. Place the apple in the processor bowl and process for 2–3 seconds, to chop. Remove and set aside.
4. Add the nuts to the processor bowl and process for 2–3 seconds, until coarsely chopped. Remove and set aside.
5. Melt the butter in a pan, add the celery and onion mixture and cook gently for 5 minutes. Add the apple and nuts and cook for 3 minutes. Add the breadcrumbs, lemon juice and salt and pepper and mix well. Place the mixture along the pork loin, roll up and tie firmly. Brush with oil and rub with salt.
6. Weigh the joint and calculate the cooking time, allowing 30 minutes per lb, plus 30 minutes. Place on a rack in a roasting pan and cook in a 350°F oven for the calculated time; raise the oven temperature to 425°F for the last 10 minutes to crisp the crackling. Keep warm while preparing the sauce.
7. Skim away any fat from the meat juices. Place the cornstarch in a small pan, gradually add the meat juices and blend well. Gradually add the apple juice and bring to the boil, stirring constantly, until smooth and thickened. Stir in the cream and salt and pepper.
8. Slice the pork and serve immediately, with the sauce and seasonal vegetables.

SWEET AND SOUR PORK BALLS

Delicious balls of pork simmered in a rich and colorful sweet and sour sauce make this dish exotic enough to serve at a dinner party, with plain boiled rice and a crisp green salad.

pared rind of ¼ orange
6 slices brown bread,
*   cubed*
1½ lb diced pork
1 large onion
dash of Tabasco sauce
1 egg
2 tablespoons salad oil
salt and pepper to taste
parsley or cilantro sprigs to
*   garnish*
FOR THE SAUCE:
1 each green, red and
*   yellow pepper, cored*
*   and seeded*

1 tablespoon cornstarch
¾ cup stock
1 tablespoon salad oil
2 tomatoes, skinned and
*   chopped*
3 tablespoons light brown
*   sugar*
1 tablespoon soy sauce
3 tablespoons red wine
*   vinegar*
¾ cup orange juice
½ teaspoon Chinese
*   5-spice powder*

Serves 6
Preparation time:
25 minutes
Cooking time:
30–35 minutes
Freezing:
Recommended

1. Fit the metal chopping blade. With the motor running, add the orange rind then the bread cubes through the feed tube and process for 5–8 seconds, to make citrus-flavored crumbs. Remove and set aside.
2. Place the pork in the processor bowl and process for 4–6 seconds, to grind.
3. Add the onion, breadcrumbs, Tabasco sauce, egg, and salt and pepper and process for 4–6 seconds, to mix. Remove the mixture and shape into about 18–20 meatballs.
4. Heat the oil in a heavy-based frying pan, add the pork balls and fry for about 10 minutes, until evenly browned.
5. Meanwhile, prepare the sauce. Place the peppers in the processor bowl and process for 4–5 seconds, to chop.
6. Place the cornstarch in a small bowl, add a little of the stock and mix until smooth. Gradually stir in the remaining stock and set aside.
7. Heat the oil in another pan, add the peppers and fry for about 5 minutes, until softened. Add the blended cornstarch with the remaining ingredients and salt and pepper. Bring to the boil, stirring, then pour over the pork balls.
8. Cover and cook gently for 20–25 minutes, until the pork balls are tender and the sauce has thickened. Garnish with parsley or cilantro to serve.

CHEESY TOAD-IN-THE-HOLES

4 oz Cheddar cheese
1 tablespoon salad oil
1 lb pork sausages

¹/₂–1 teaspoon prepared
*   mustard*
1¹/₄ cups Basic Batter*
sage leaves to garnish

1. Fit the grating disc and grate the cheese.
2. Divide the oil and sausages between 8 small ramekins or place in 1 large 8 × 12 inch shallow ovenproof dish. Cook in a 425°F oven for 10 minutes (if using cocktail sausages, cook for only 5 minutes). Lower the oven temperature to 400°F.
3. Add the mustard and half the cheese to the batter, pour around the sausages and sprinkle with remaining cheese.
4. Bake for 20–30 minutes, until well risen, crisp and golden brown. Serve immediately, garnished with sage.

Serves 4
Preparation time:
10 minutes, plus making batter
Cooking time:
25–40 minutes
Freezing:
Not recommended

PORK AND KUMQUAT CURRY

Kumquats add elegance to this curry, but if unavailable substitute thin-skinned tangerines or the cubed flesh of a peeled mango.

1 1/2 lb pork fillet
1 large onion
2 tablespoons salad oil
2 bay leaves
2 cardamoms
6 cloves
6 black peppercorns
1/2 teaspoon ground cumin
1 cinnamon stick
2 tablespoons tomato paste
1 cup stock
1 cup orange juice

1/2 lb kumquats, quartered
FOR THE CURRY PASTE:
1 onion
1 clove garlic
1 tablespoon coriander
  seeds
1 teaspoon ground ginger
1 teaspoon ground red
  pepper
2 teaspoons garam masala
1 1/2 teaspoons turmeric

Serves 4–6
Preparation time:
20–25 minutes
Cooking time:
45–50 minutes
Freezing:
Recommended for up to 1 month

1. First, make the curry paste. Fit the metal chopping blade. Place all the ingredients in the processor bowl and process for about 20 seconds, to puree. Set aside.
2. Fit the slicing disc and slice the onion.
3. Cut the pork into cubes. Heat the oil in a flameproof casserole, add the onion and pork and cook over a high heat for about 10 minutes, until evenly browned.
4. Add the bay leaves, cardamoms, cloves, peppercorns, cumin, cinnamon stick, tomato paste, stock and orange juice and mix well. Cover and simmer for 10 minutes.
5. Stir in the kumquats and curry paste, blending well. Cover and simmer for 25–30 minutes, until very tender.
6. Serve with Basmati rice and a cucumber salad.

TURKEY BREASTS SURPRISE

Turkey breasts are an economical way of buying prime turkey meat for a popular family supper dish.

4 slices day-old bread,
  cubed
bouquet garni
3 oz Cheddar cheese
4 turkey breasts
4 slices ham

4 teaspoons coarse-grain
  mustard
1 egg, beaten
1/4 cup butter
1 tablespoon salad oil
salt and pepper to taste
thyme sprigs to garnish

1. Fit the metal chopping blade. With the motor running, add the bread cubes through the feed tube and process for about 5 seconds, to make fine dry breadcrumbs. Add the herbs, and salt and pepper and process for about 1 second, to mix. Place in a shallow dish.

2. Fit the grating disc and grate the cheese.

3. Flatten the turkey breasts by hitting with a rolling pin or meat mallet. Spread one side of each breast with mustard, top with grated cheese and cover with a slice of ham.

4. Carefully dip the turkey breasts into the beaten egg, then coat in the breadcrumbs, patting well to seal.

5. Heat the butter and oil in a heavy-based frying pan, add the turkey breasts and fry for about 15 minutes, turning once, until golden and cooked through. Drain on paper towels.

6. Garnish with thyme and serve immediately, with baked tomatoes or Vegetable Mirepoix (page 34).

Serves 4
Preparation time:
20 minutes
Cooking time:
15 minutes
Freezing:
Recommended at end of stage 4; thaw thoroughly before cooking

VEGETABLES TAJ MAHAL

Fresh coconut gives this a wonderful flavor; but you could use 1 cup unsweetened flaked coconut, blended with ¾ cup hot milk, to replace coconut and water.

2 inch piece fresh root ginger	*1½ teaspoons turmeric*
2 cloves garlic	*2 teaspoons garam masala*
1 onion	*1 tablespoon ground coriander*
1 green chili, seeded	*¾ cup green beans*
2 carrots	*¼ lb cauliflower florets*
2 celery sticks	*2 potatoes, diced*
1 small eggplant, quartered	*2 oz okra*
1 green pepper, cored and seeded	*2 oz pearl onions*
¼ cup salad oil	*1 teaspoon salt*
1 teaspoon mustard seeds, crushed	*½ lb fresh coconut flesh*
	¾ cup water

Serves 4
Preparation time:
20 minutes
Cooking time:
About 45 minutes
Freezing:
Recommended for
up to 1 month

1. Fit the metal chopping blade. Place the ginger, garlic, onion and chili in the processor bowl and process for 8–10 seconds, until finely chopped. Remove and set aside.
2. Fit the slicing disc and slice the carrots, celery, eggplant and green pepper. Remove and set aside.
3. Heat the oil in a large pan, add the mustard seeds and fry for 1 minute. Stir in the onion mixture and fry gently for 10 minutes. Add the turmeric, garam masala and coriander and cook for 2 minutes. Add all the vegetables, stir well and cook gently for 5 minutes.
4. Meanwhile, fit the metal chopping blade. Place the salt, coconut and water in the processor bowl and process for about 20 seconds, to puree. Add to the vegetable mixture, cover and simmer for 25 minutes.
5. Spoon into a warmed serving dish. Serve with Basmati rice, poppadoms, yogurt and mango pickle.

BACON GOUGÈRE

3 oz Cheddar cheese	*2-egg quantity Choux Pastry**
1 onion	
⅓ lb cooked bacon or ham	*2 tablespoons fresh breadcrumbs (see page 7)*
¼ lb mushrooms	
1 tablespoon salad oil	*salt and pepper to taste*

1. Fit the grating disc and grate the cheese. Remove and set aside.

2. Fit the metal chopping blade. Place the onion and bacon or ham in the processor bowl and process for 3–4 seconds, until coarsely chopped. Set aside.

3. Fit the slicing disc and slice the mushrooms.

4. Heat the oil in a pan, add the onion mixture, mushrooms, and salt and pepper, and cook gently for 8–10 minutes, stirring occasionally.

5. Add ½ cup of the cheese to the choux pastry and process for 5–10 seconds, to mix.

6. Spoon half of the pastry into a greased 1½ quart ovenproof dish or, for individual portions, divide between 4 large scallop shells. Spoon the bacon mixture into the center.

7. Spoon or pipe the remaining pastry around the edge and sprinkle with the remaining cheese. Sprinkle the bacon filling with the breadcrumbs.

8. Bake in a 400°F oven for 40–45 minutes; for individual dishes bake for 25–30 minutes. Serve immediately.

Serves 4
Preparation time: 30 minutes, plus making pastry
Cooking time: 25–45 minutes
Freezing: Not recommended

SHRIMP AND WATERCRESS QUICHE

*8 oz Lemon Basic Pastry**
1 small onion
1 bunch watercress
1 tablespoon butter
3 extra large eggs, beaten

⅔ cup whipping cream
2 teaspoons dry mustard
¼ lb shelled medium-size
  shrimp
salt and pepper to taste

Serves 4–6
Preparation time:
20–25 minutes
plus making pastry
Cooking time:
35–40 minutes
Freezing:
Not recommended

1. Roll out the prepared pastry on a lightly floured surface and use to line a 9 inch loose-bottomed tart plate. Line with waxed paper and fill with baking beans. Bake 'blind' in a 375°F oven for 15 minutes. Lower the temperature to 350°F.
2. Meanwhile, fit the metal chopping blade. Place the onion and watercress in the processor bowl and process for about 5 seconds, to chop.
3. Melt the butter in a pan, add the onion and watercress and cook gently for 5 minutes. Remove from the heat, leave to cool slightly, then stir in the eggs, cream, mustard, and salt and pepper.
4. Remove the waxed paper and beans from the quiche case and sprinkle the shrimp over the base. Pour in the watercress mixture. Return to the oven and bake for 20–25 minutes until firm. Remove the quiche from the plate.
5. Serve warm or cold with a mixed salad, for a special family lunch or supper dish.

TURKEY PICNIC PIE

A veal, ham and turkey pie makes a splendid centerpiece for any cold spread. Serve on a picnic, as part of a cold buffet, or as a lunchbox item.

½ lb cubed veal
½ lb cooked ham
1 onion
pinch of ground mace or
  grated nutmeg
¾ lb Hot Water Crust
  *Pastry**

2 cups diced cooked turkey
salt and pepper to taste
beaten egg or milk to glaze
FOR THE JELLIED STOCK:
1¼ cups chicken stock
1 envelope gelatin

1. Fit the metal chopping blade. Place the veal, ham, onion, mace or nutmeg, and salt and pepper in the processor bowl and process for 15–20 seconds, to chop finely or grind.

2. Roll out two-thirds of the pastry on a lightly floured surface and use to line a greased 6 inch round loose-bottomed cake pan or small game pie mold.

3. Place half of the veal mixture in the pan, cover with the turkey and top with the remaining veal mixture.

4. Roll out the remaining pastry to make a lid. Dampen the pastry rim and cover with the lid. Trim, seal and flute the edges. Use any pastry trimmings to decorate the pie as you wish. Make a hole in the top of the pie and place on a baking sheet. Brush with beaten egg or milk.

5. Bake in a 400°F oven for 30 minutes. Lower the temperature to 325°F, glaze again and bake for 1–1¼ hours. Leave in the pan to cool.

6. To make the jellied stock, place the stock and gelatin in a pan and heat gently until dissolved. Season with salt and pepper, leave to cool, then pour gradually through a funnel into the pie through the hole in the lid. Chill overnight. Remove from the pan to serve.

Serves 8
Preparation time:
20–30 minutes
plus making pastry
and chilling
Cooking time:
1½–1¾ hours
Freezing:
Not recommended

SUPPER PIZZAS

FOR THE BASE:
2 cups self-rising flour
1 teaspoon salt
2 tablespoons butter
²/₃ cup milk or milk and
  water mixed
FOR THE TOPPING:
1 onion
1 teaspoon dried oregano
1 teaspoon dried basil
1 teaspoon sugar
2 × 14 oz cans tomatoes,
  drained
8 oz Mozzarella cheese
4 teaspoons mustard
16 slices salami
4 black olives
salt and pepper to taste

Serves 4
Preparation time:
25–30 minutes
Cooking time:
15 minutes
Freezing:
Recommended at
end of stage 6

1. To make the base, fit the metal chopping blade. Place the flour, salt and butter in the processor bowl and process for 5–7 seconds, until the mixture resembles breadcrumbs.
2. With the motor running, add the milk through the feed tube and process for about 4 seconds, until the mixture forms a smooth dough.
3. Divide the dough into 4 pieces and roll each piece out on a lightly floured surface to a 6 inch circle. Place on baking sheets.
4. To make the topping, place the onion in the processor bowl and process for 2–3 seconds, to chop. Place in a pan with the herbs, sugar, tomatoes, and salt and pepper and stir well. Cook for about 15 minutes, until thickened.
5. Meanwhile, fit the grating disc and grate the cheese.
6. Spread 1 teaspoon of the mustard over each pizza base and top with a quarter of the tomato mixture. Cover each with 4 salami slices and sprinkle with a quarter of the cheese. Top each pizza with an olive.
7. Brush with a little olive oil and bake in a 450°F oven for about 15 minutes, until golden and bubbling. Serve piping hot with a green salad.

VARIATIONS

Seafood Supper Pizzas: Prepare as above but replace the salami and olives with 16 canned sardines or 16 anchovy fillets and 6 oz shelled medium-size shrimp.

Vegetable Supper Pizzas: Prepare as above but replace the salami with 1 lb frozen stir-fry vegetables.

Mushroom and Ham Supper Pizzas: Prepare as above but replace the salami and olives with 2½ cups chopped ham and ¾ lb sliced mushrooms. Sprinkle with a little chopped oregano before cooking.

LAYERED POTATOES DAUPHINOISE

2 lb potatoes
1 large onion
1/4 cup butter

2 cups milk
salt and pepper to taste
parsley sprigs to garnish

Serves 4
Preparation time:
15 minutes
Cooking time:
1½–2 hours
Freezing:
Not recommended

1. Fit the slicing disc and slice the potatoes and onion.
2. Lightly grease the base and sides of a large shallow ovenproof dish with some of the butter. Place a layer of potato and onion in the dish, dot with a little butter and sprinkle generously with salt and pepper. Repeat the layers until all the potato and onion has been used. Dot the top with butter.
3. Bring the milk just to the boil, then pour over the potato mixture. Cover with foil and bake in a 375°F oven for 1½–2 hours, removing the foil for the final 45 minutes.
4. Garnish with parsley to serve.

MINTED RATATOUILLE

2 onions
1 green pepper, cored and
    seeded
1 red or yellow pepper,
    cored and seeded
1/2 lb zucchini
1 eggplant, quartered

1/4 lb mushrooms
1/4 cup olive oil
1 lb tomatoes, skinned,
    seeded and quartered
1 tablespoon chopped mint
salt and pepper to taste
mint sprigs to garnish

Serves 4
Preparation time:
20 minutes
Cooking time:
About 1 hour
Freezing:
Recommended

1. Fit the slicing disc and slice the onions, peppers, zucchini and eggplant. Remove and set aside.
2. Slice the mushrooms through the disc and set aside in a separate bowl.
3. Heat the oil in a flameproof casserole, add the onion mixture and fry for about 10 minutes, until softened.
4. Stir in the tomatoes, cover and simmer for 20 minutes.
5. Add the mushrooms, mint, and salt and pepper and stir well. Simmer, uncovered, for about 30 minutes, or until the vegetables are tender but retain their shape.
6. Garnish with mint and serve hot or cold.

VEGETABLE MIREPOIX WITH CITRUS BUTTER

Crisp green vegetables with contrasting flavors and textures make a welcome accompaniment when tossed in a herby lemon butter.

2 celery sticks	*1 sprig each parsley, mint,*
2 small zucchini	*tarragon and marjoram*
1/2 large cucumber	*1 teaspoon snipped chives*
3/4 cup green beans	*2 teaspoons lemon juice*
1/4 lb snow peas	*1/4 cup butter*

Serves 4
Preparation time:
15–20 minutes
Cooking time:
5–6 minutes
Freezing:
Not recommended

1. Fit the slicing disc and slice the celery, zucchini and cucumber. Place in a saucepan.
2. Fit the metal chopping blade. Place the green beans in the processor bowl and process for 1–2 seconds, until coarsely chopped. Add to the pan with the snow peas.
3. Cook the vegetables in boiling salted water for 5–6 minutes, until tender but still crisp. Drain thoroughly.
4. Meanwhile, with the motor running, add the herb sprigs through the feed tube and process for about 5 seconds, to chop. Add the chives, lemon juice and butter and process for 8–10 seconds, to blend.
5. Spoon over the hot vegetables and toss well to coat. Serve immediately.

CREAMED SPRING VEGETABLES

A selection of creamed spring vegetables often makes more interesting and enjoyable eating than just boiled vegetables. For a quick, light supper dish, top with grated cheese and broil until golden and bubbly; serve with crusty bread.

1/4 lb baby carrots	*1/4 onion*
1/4 lb baby turnips	*2 tablespoons butter*
2 celery sticks	*1/4 cup all-purpose flour*
1 large leek	*11/4 cups milk*
1/4 lb white cabbage	*salt and pepper to taste*
1/4 lb snow peas	*parsley sprigs to garnish*
2 parsley sprigs	

1. Fit the slicing disc and slice the carrots, turnips, celery and leek. Place in a saucepan and cook in boiling salted water for 10 minutes.

2. Meanwhile, slice the cabbage through the disc. Add to the vegetable mixture with the snow peas and cook for 5 minutes. Drain thoroughly.

3. Meanwhile, fit the metal chopping blade. Place the parsley and onion in the processor bowl and process for 3–4 seconds, until finely chopped.

4. Melt the butter in a pan, add the onion and parsley and cook for 3 minutes. Stir in the flour and cook for 1 minute. Gradually add the milk, bring to the boil, stirring, and cook for 2 minutes. Add the vegetables and toss to coat.

5. Season with salt and pepper and spoon into a warmed serving dish. Serve immediately, garnished with parsley.

Serves 4–6
Preparation time:
20 minutes
Cooking time:
About 15 minutes
Freezing:
Recommended

VEGETABLE PUREES

1 lb parsnips	*GARLIC AND HERB*
1 lb carrots	* BUTTER:*
1 lb broccoli	*1 clove garlic*
¼ cup grated Cheddar	*1 parsley sprig*
* cheese (optional)*	*¼ cup butter*
BLUE CHEESE BUTTER:	*LEMON AND PARSLEY*
¼ cup butter	* BUTTER:*
2 oz blue Stilton or Danish	*grated rind of ¼ lemon*
* Blue cheese*	*1 parsley sprig*
salt and pepper to taste	*¼ cup butter*

Serves 4–6
Preparation time:
30–40 minutes
Cooking time:
10 minutes
Freezing:
Recommended

1. Fit the slicing disc and slice the parsnips. Set aside.
2. Slice the carrots through the disc. Set aside.
3. Split the broccoli into equal-sized spears.
4. Cook the vegetables in separate pans of boiling salted water for about 10 minutes, until tender; drain.
5. Meanwhile, prepare the butters. To prepare the blue cheese butter, fit the metal chopping blade. Place all the ingredients in the processor bowl and process for about 10 seconds, to blend, scraping down the bowl once. Remove and set aside. Wash the processor bowl.
6. To make the garlic and herb butter, fit the metal chopping blade. Place the garlic and parsley in the processor bowl and process for 5–8 seconds, until finely chopped. Add the butter, and salt and pepper to taste and process for 10 seconds, to blend, scraping down the bowl once. Remove and set aside. Wash the processor bowl.
7. To make the lemon and parsley butter, fit the metal chopping blade. Place the lemon rind and parsley in the processor bowl and process for 5–8 seconds, until finely chopped. Add the butter, and salt and pepper to taste and process for about 10 seconds, to blend, scraping down the bowl once. Add the broccoli and process for 3–5 seconds, to puree. Remove and keep warm.
8. Place the parsnips and blue cheese butter in the processor bowl and process for about 5 seconds, to puree. Remove and keep warm.
9. Place the carrots and garlic and herb butter in the processor bowl and process for about 5 seconds, to puree.
10. Serve the vegetable purees in 3 separate warmed dishes, or arrange in a warmed round serving dish to form 3 triangles of color. Mark the surface with a fork.
11. If you wish, sprinkle with the cheese and broil until golden. Serve immediately.

ITALIAN MUSHROOM SALAD

It is essential to use fresh Parmesan cheese for this side salad or appetizer dish. Slice with the processor slicing disc if your handbook states this is possible, with the special Parmesan cheese grater disc if your model has one, or shave with a sharp knife.

½ lb small mushrooms
4 oz Parmesan cheese
chopped parsley to garnish

FOR THE VINAIGRETTE:
2 tablespoons lemon juice
1 soft-boiled egg yolk
½ cup salad oil
salt and pepper to taste

Serves 4
Preparation time:
20 minutes
Freezing:
Not recommended

1. Fit the slicing disc and slice the mushrooms. Arrange on a shallow serving plate. Slice the Parmesan (see above) and sprinkle on top.
2. To make the vinaigrette, fit the metal chopping blade. Place the lemon juice, egg yolk, and salt and pepper in the processor bowl and process for about 5 seconds, to blend.
3. With the motor running, pour the oil through the feed tube and process for 4–5 seconds, to make a thickened vinaigrette.
4. Spoon over the salad and sprinkle with parsley. Serve with warm crusty bread.

CUCUMBER AND ZUCCHINI SALAD

A deviled herby vegetable salad, good with cold meats, game pies and other buffet fare. Make at the last possible moment for absolute freshness.

3 small zucchini
½ small cucumber
chopped pine nuts to
*   garnish*
FOR THE DRESSING:
6 basil leaves

¼ cup salad oil
2 tablespoons white wine
*   vinegar*
1 teaspoon wholegrain
*   mustard*
salt and pepper to taste

1. Fit the grating disc and grate the zucchini and cucumber. Place in a bowl.
2. To make the dressing, fit the metal chopping blade. Place the basil in the processor bowl and process for 2–3 seconds, to chop.
3. Add the oil, vinegar, mustard, and salt and pepper and process for about 3 seconds, to blend.
4. Pour over the cucumber and zucchini and toss to mix.
5. Spoon into a shallow serving dish and sprinkle with chopped pine nuts. Serve immediately.

Serves 4
Preparation time:
10 minutes
Freezing:
Not recommended

WALDORF CELERY CRUNCH

*1 each red and green
    dessert apple, cored and
    quartered
5 celery sticks
1/2 cup roasted salted
    peanuts
15 oz can baby corn cobs,
    drained
1 tablespoon snipped
    chives*

*FOR THE DRESSING:
2 tablespoons sour cream
2 tablespoons plain yogurt
3 tablespoons pineapple
    juice
1 teaspoon dried oregano
pepper to taste*

**Serves 4
Preparation time:**
10–15 minutes
Freezing:
Not recommended

1. Fit the slicing disc and slice the apples and celery. Place in a bowl.
2. Fit the metal chopping blade. Place the peanuts in the processor bowl and process for 2–3 seconds, until coarsely chopped. Add to the apple and celery with the corn cobs and chives, stirring well to mix.
3. To make the dressing, place all the ingredients in the processor bowl and process for 2–3 seconds, to blend. Pour over the salad and toss lightly. Serve immediately.

ROSY COLESLAW

*1 small red cabbage, cored
    and quartered
2 red or green dessert
    apples, cored and
    quartered
2 celery sticks
3 carrots*

*1/3 cup walnut pieces
1/3 cup raisins
2/3 cup Mayonnaise*
1/4 cup plain yogurt
salt and ground red pepper
    to taste*

**Serves 6–8
Preparation time:**
10–15 minutes
Freezing:
Not recommended

1. Fit the slicing disc and slice the cabbage. Place in a serving bowl. Slice the apples and celery through the disc; add to the bowl.
2. Fit the grating disc and grate the carrots. Add to the cabbage mixture with the walnuts and raisins and mix well.
3. Fit the metal chopping or plastic blending blade. Place the mayonnaise, yogurt, and salt and ground red pepper in the processor bowl and process for about 2 seconds, to blend.
4. Spoon over the coleslaw and toss well to coat. Serve as soon as possible.

CURRIED CHICKEN DISCOVERY

¹/₂ cucumber
1 lb crisp eating apples,
*   cored and quartered*
1 large fennel, quartered
2 tablespoons lemon juice
2¹/₂ lb chicken, cooked and
*   skinned*

FOR THE DRESSING:
1 quantity Mayonnaise*,
*   made with lemon juice*
2 teaspoons curry paste
2 tablespoons apple puree
¹/₃ cup sour cream
salt and pepper to taste
TO SERVE:
lettuce or Belgium endive
*   leaves*

1. Fit the slicing disc and slice the cucumber, apples and fennel. Place in a bowl. Add the lemon juice and toss well. Remove the meat from the chicken, dice and add to the salad; mix well and set aside.

2. Line a serving plate with lettuce or Belgium endive leaves.

3. To make the dressing, fit the metal chopping or plastic blending blade. Place all the ingredients in the processor bowl and process for 3–5 seconds, to mix.

4. Add to the chicken salad, toss carefully, then pile on top of the lettuce or Belgium endive. Serve immediately.

Serves 6
Preparation time:
25 minutes
Freezing:
Not recommended

DELICATESSEN SAUSAGE SALAD

A look down the delicatessen counter will be all the inspiration you need to mix and match the vast array of sausages in this quickly made main meal salad.

2 frankfurters
1/2 lb mixed delicatessen
* sausage, e.g. peperoni,*
* salami, chorizo,*
* bierwurst, mortadella*
2 firm ripe pears, peeled
* and quartered*
4 oz Gruyère cheese
chopped parsley to garnish

FOR THE DRESSING:
2 tiny sour gherkins
1 tablespoon cider or wine
* vinegar*
2 teaspoons lemon juice
3 tablespoons salad oil
1/2 teaspoon Dijon mustard
salt and pepper to taste

Serves 4
Preparation time:
10–15 minutes
Freezing:
Not recommended

1. Fit the slicing disc and slice the frankfurters. Place in a serving bowl with the other sliced meats.
2. Slice the pears through the disc and add to the sausage mixture.
3. Fit the grating disc and grate the cheese. Add to the sausage mixture.
4. To make the dressing, fit the metal chopping blade. Place the gherkins in the processor bowl and process for about 2 seconds, to chop. Add the remaining ingredients and process for 1–2 seconds, to blend.
5. Pour over the salad and toss quickly to mix. Sprinkle with parsley and serve immediately, with crusty bread.

DANISH BLUE DRESSING

A superb blue cheese dressing ideal for salads and sandwich fillings, and for spooning onto baked potatoes.

4 oz Danish blue cheese
1/4 cup Mayonnaise*
1/3 cup plain yogurt

pepper to taste
snipped chives to garnish

Makes 1 1/4 cups
Preparation time:
5 minutes
Freezing:
Not recommended

1. Fit the metal chopping or plastic blending blade. Place the cheese, mayonnaise and yogurt in the processor bowl and process for 8–10 seconds, until smooth and creamy. Transfer to a serving bowl.
2. Season with pepper and chill until required. Sprinkle with chives to serve.

THOUSAND ISLAND DRESSING

1 shallot
2 tiny sour gherkins
¹/₂ each small green and
   red pepper
10 stuffed green olives
2 cups Mayonnaise*

1 tablespoon tomato
   catsup
¹/₄ teaspoon garlic puree
   (see page 6)
few drops of chili sauce
salt and pepper to taste
few olive slices to garnish

1. Fit the metal chopping blade. Place the shallot, gherkins, peppers and olives in the processor bowl and process for 3–5 seconds, to chop.
2. Add the mayonnaise, tomato catsup, garlic puree, chili sauce, and salt and pepper, and process for 1–2 seconds, to blend.
3. Spoon into a serving dish and top with olive slices. Chill lightly.
4. Serve with salads, as a topping for baked potatoes, or as a hamburger relish.

Makes 2¹/₂ cups
Preparation time:
10 minutes
Freezing:
Not recommended

DESSERTS

HUMBLE PLUM CRUMBLE

*1½ lb tart plums, halved,
    pitted and quartered
2 tablespoons orange juice
¼ cup dark brown sugar,
    packed
1½ cups whole wheat or
    all-purpose flour*

*1 teaspoon ground
    cinnamon (optional)
¼ cup butter
¼ cup light brown
    granulated sugar*

**Serves 4
Preparation time:**
15 minutes
Cooking time:
30 minutes
Freezing:
Recommended

1. Mix the plums with the orange juice and dark brown sugar to taste in a 1½ quart ovenproof dish.
2. Fit the metal chopping blade. Place the flour, cinnamon, if using, and butter in the processor bowl and process for about 6 seconds, until the mixture resembles fine breadcrumbs. Add the light brown sugar and process for about 2 seconds, to mix.
3. Spoon over the plums, leveling the surface. Bake in a 375°F oven for 30 minutes, until golden.
4. Serve hot with ice cream or whipped cream.

CHERRY KISSEL

*15 oz can black cherries,
    drained and pitted
2 tablespoons white wine*

*1 tablespoon lemon juice
1¼ cups custard
⅔ cup heavy cream*

**Serves 4
Preparation time:**
10–15 minutes
plus chilling
Freezing:
Not recommended

1. Fit the metal chopping blade. Place the cherries, wine and lemon juice in the processor bowl and process for 20–30 seconds, until smooth.
2. Add the custard and process for about 5 seconds, to mix with the cherry puree. Pour into a large serving dish or individual glass dishes.
3. Whip the cream until soft peaks form, using the processor whipping blade if your model has one. Swirl into the cherry mixture to give a streaked appearance. Alternatively, pipe lines of cream onto individual servings and draw a skewer across the lines in alternate directions to create a feathered pattern. Chill thoroughly before serving.

BOYSENBERRY MOUSSE

When boysenberries are unavailable use raspberries instead, to make an equally delicious mousse.

3/4 lb boysenberries
1/4 cup orange juice
1/4–1/3 cup superfine sugar
  (depending on
  sweetness of the fruit)
2 eggs plus 1 yolk

1 envelope gelatin
1 1/4 cups heavy cream,
  whipped
berry leaves to decorate
  (optional)

Serves 6
Preparation time:
15–20 minutes
plus chilling
Cooking time:
5 minutes
Freezing:
Recommended

1. Place the boysenberries and 1 tablespoon of the orange juice in a pan and cook gently for about 5 minutes, until just soft. Leave to cool slightly.
2. Fit the metal chopping blade. Pour the boysenberry mixture into the processor bowl and process for 5–6 seconds, until smooth. Sieve to remove the pits.
3. Beat the sugar, eggs and egg yolk together until thick; this can be done in the processor if your model has a whipping blade.
4. Sprinkle the gelatin over the remaining orange juice and leave to soften. Heat gently until dissolved, then fold into the egg mixture with the boysenberry puree and half of the cream. Spoon into a serving dish and chill until set.
5. Decorate with swirls of the remaining cream and berry leaves, if available.

LEMON AND KIWI CHEESECAKE

5 oz graham crackers
1/3 cup butter
pared rind of 1 lemon
3/4 cup low fat Ricotta or
  sieved cottage cheese
1/4 cup superfine sugar
2 eggs, separated

1 envelope gelatin
1/4 cup lemon juice
2 tablespoons cold water
1/2 lemon or plain yogurt
2/3 cup heavy cream
4 kiwi fruit, peeled
1 lemon

1. Grease and line a 9 inch loose-bottomed cake pan.
2. Fit the metal chopping blade. Break the graham crackers into the processor bowl and process for 3–5 seconds, to make crumbs.
3. Melt the butter in a pan, stir in the crumbs and mix well. Press onto the base of the prepared pan and chill until set.
4. Place the lemon rind in the processor bowl and process

for 4–5 seconds, until finely chopped. Add the soft cheese, sugar and egg yolks and process for 5–8 seconds, to blend.

5. Sprinkle the gelatin over the lemon juice and water and leave to soften, then heat gently until dissolved. Add to the cheese mixture with the yogurt and process for about 2 seconds, to blend. Transfer to a bowl and chill until just beginning to set at the edge. Wash the processor bowl.

6. Whip the cream until soft peaks form, using the processor whipping blade if your model has one. Fold into the cheesecake mixture with a metal spoon.

7. Coarsely chop one of the kiwi fruit and fold into the cheesecake mixture.

8. Beat the egg whites until stiff peaks form, then fold into the cheesecake mixture with a metal spoon. Quickly pour onto the graham cracker crust and chill until set.

9. Fit the slicing disc. Halve the lemon and slice through the disc. Slice the remaining kiwi fruit through the disc.

10. To serve, remove the cheesecake from the pan and carefully peel away the waxed paper. Decorate the top with the lemon and kiwi slices.

Serves 6–8
Preparation time:
30 minutes, plus chilling
Freezing:
Recommended at end of stage 8

PINK PLUM CHIFFON

One of the simplest yet most attractive desserts I know. For maximum effect, spread the cream over the chiffon and arrange the brandy snaps on top.

1 lb 4 oz can red plums in syrup, drained and pitted
1 package raspberry gelatin dessert

1/2 cup boiling water
1 1/4 cups heavy cream, whipped
whipped cream to decorate
12 brandy snaps

Serves 6
Preparation time:
15 minutes, plus chilling
Freezing:
Recommended

1. Fit the metal chopping blade. Place the drained plums in the processor bowl and process for 5–6 seconds, to puree.
2. Dissolve the gelatin in the boiling water and mix with the plum puree. Chill until just beginning to set.
3. Return to the processor bowl with the whipped cream and process for 8–10 seconds, until foaming. Pour the mixture into a 7½ × 3½ × 2½ inch loaf pan and chill until set.
4. To serve, dip briefly into hot water and turn out onto a serving dish. Decorate with swirls of whipped cream and serve immediately, with brandy snaps.

ICE CREAM PROFITEROLES

2-egg quantity Sweet
  Choux Pastry*
about 1 1/4 cups chocolate,
  vanilla or coffee ice
  cream, softened

CHOCOLATE SAUCE:
6 oz baker's semi-sweet
  chocolate
1/2 cup water
1/2 cup sugar

1. Place the choux pastry in a piping bag fitted with a large plain tip and pipe small mounds onto a greased baking sheet.
2. Bake in a 425°F oven for 10 minutes. Lower the temperature to 375°F and bake for 20–25 minutes, until golden. Make a slit in the side of each bun to allow any steam to escape and cool on a rack.
3. Meanwhile, make the chocolate sauce. Place the chocolate and 3 tablespoons of the water in a pan and heat gently until melted. Add the remaining water and the sugar, blending well, and simmer, uncovered, until the chocolate coats the back of the spoon. Leave to cool.
4. Carefully spoon the ice cream into the choux buns and pile onto a serving dish. Spoon over the chocolate sauce and serve immediately.

Serves 4
Preparation time:
20–25 minutes
plus making pastry
Cooking time:
30–35 minutes
Freezing:
Recommended;
freeze unfilled
choux buns, ice
cream and
chocolate sauce
separately

LEMON SAUCE PUDDING

A delicious tangy lemon pudding that separates into two distinctive layers after cooking—one a light lemon sponge cake and the other a lemon sauce.

2 tablespoons butter
1/3 cup superfine sugar
grated rind and juice of 1
*   large lemon*

2 eggs, separated
1/2 cup self-rising flour
2/3 cup milk

Serves 4
Preparation time:
15 minutes
Cooking time:
35 minutes
Freezing:
Not recommended

1. Fit the metal chopping or plastic blending blade. Place the butter, sugar, lemon rind and juice, egg yolks, flour and milk in the processor bowl and process for 8–10 seconds, to mix.
2. Beat the egg whites until stiff. Fold into the lemon mixture with a metal spoon.
3. Pour into a 1 quart ovenproof dish and place in a roasting pan containing warm water to come about half-way up the dish.
4. Bake in a 375°F oven for 35 minutes. Serve immediately, with cream if wished.

PEACH SHORTCAKE GATEAU

An elegant home-baked gateau. For a change, use other soft fruits in season. Best eaten on the day it is made.

1/3 cup blanched almonds
2 1/2 cups all-purpose flour
1/3 cup ground rice
1 cup butter
1/2 cup superfine sugar
finely grated rind of 1
*   lemon*
1 egg yolk
3 tablespoons milk
mint sprigs to decorate

FOR THE FILLING AND
*   TOPPING:*
1 quantity Whipped Danish
*   Cream**
1 tablespoon powdered
*   sugar*
1 lb small peaches, peeled
*   and halved*

1. Fit the metal chopping blade. Place the almonds in the processor bowl and process for about 3 seconds, until coarsely chopped. Remove and set aside.
2. Place the flour, ground rice and butter in the processor bowl and process for about 5 seconds, until the mixture resembles fine breadcrumbs.
3. Add the almonds and remaining ingredients and process for about 4 seconds, to make a firm but pliable dough.

4. Roll out the dough on a lightly floured surface to a 10 × 7 inch rectangle. Cut in half to give two 10 × 3½ inch rectangles.

5. Place the rectangles on 1 or 2 greased baking sheets and bake in a 350°F oven for 20–25 minutes. Cut one rectangle into 6 or 8 slices while still warm. Cool on a rack.

6. Meanwhile, prepare the filling and topping. Wash the processor bowl. Whip the cream with the powdered sugar until soft peaks form (using the processor whipping blade if your model has one). Set aside a quarter for decoration.

7. Fit the metal chopping blade. Reserve 2 peach halves for decoration. Place the rest in the processor bowl and process for barely 1–2 seconds, until coarsely chopped. Fold into the cream.

8. Place the whole shortcake rectangle on a serving plate and spread with the peach mixture. Arrange the small shortcake slices on top.

9. Place the reserved cream in a piping bag fitted with a star-shaped tip and pipe a swirl of cream on each piece of shortcake.

10. Slice the reserved peach halves. Decorate the short-cake with the peach slices and mint.

Serves 6–8
Preparation time: 25 minutes, plus making cream
Cooking time: 20–25 minutes
Freezing: Recommended at end of stage 5

STRAWBERRY SHORTCAKE

2 cups self-rising flour
⅓ cup sweet butter
¼ cup superfine sugar
grated rind of 1 lemon
1 egg, beaten

2–3 tablespoons milk
1 quantity Whipped Danish Cream*
4 cups sliced strawberries
mint leaves to decorate

Serves 6
Preparation time:
15 minutes, plus
making cream
Cooking time:
15–20 minutes
Freezing:
Recommended

1. Fit the metal chopping blade. Place the flour and butter in the processor bowl and process for about 5 seconds, until the mixture resembles fine breadcrumbs.

2. Add the sugar, lemon rind, egg and enough milk to process to a firm but pliable dough; process for about 4 seconds.

3. Press the mixture into a greased deep 9 inch fluted tart pan and level the surface. Bake just above the center of a 425°F oven for 15–20 minutes, until pale golden. Leave to cool in the pan for 2–3 minutes, then turn out and transfer to a rack to cool.

4. Whip the cream until soft peaks form (using the processor whipping blade if your model has one) and pipe or spoon attractively over the cooled shortcake. Top with the strawberries and mint sprigs to serve.

VICTORIAN ICE CREAM

A popular old-fashioned favorite—a brown bread and banana concoction in a rum-flavored cream.

8 slices brown bread,
*   cubed*
2 ripe bananas
3/4 cup powdered sugar

1 tablespoon rum
2 eggs, separated
2/3 cup whipping cream
1 1/4 cups heavy cream

1. Fit the metal chopping blade. With the motor running, add the bread cubes through the feed tube and process for 5–8 seconds, to make crumbs. Remove and set aside.

2. Place the bananas, powdered sugar, rum, egg yolks and whipping cream in the processor bowl and process for 8–10 seconds, until smooth.

3. Whip the heavy cream until soft peaks form, using the processor whipping blade if your model has one, then fold into the banana mixture with the breadcrumbs.

4. Beat the egg whites until stiff, then fold into the mixture with a metal spoon. Pour into a rigid freezerproof container and freeze for 3–4 hours, until firm.

5. Transfer to the refrigerator 20 minutes before serving to soften. Scoop into chilled glasses and serve with crisp dessert cookies.

Serves 4–6
Preparation time: 15 minutes, plus freezing
Freezing: Recommended

STRAWBERRY MOUSSE GARLAND

An elegant dessert that makes a stunning centerpiece for a summer buffet. Make 1–2 days ahead for perfect results.

*3-egg quantity Victoria
    Sandwich Cake Mixture**
3 cups strawberries
*2 tablespoons powdered
    sugar*
2 tablespoons Cointreau
*1½ teaspoons gelatin,
    soaked in 3 tablespoons
    orange juice*

1 egg white
*⅓ cup heavy cream,
    whipped*
*2 oz baker's semi-sweet
    chocolate*
powdered sugar to dust
FOR THE MELBA SAUCE:
1 cup raspberries
*¼ cup sifted powdered
    sugar*

Serves 8
Preparation time:
About 45 minutes,
plus making cake
mixture and
chilling
Cooking time:
About 40 minutes
Freezing:
Recommended;
freeze cake and
sauce separately

1. Spoon the cake mixture into a greased 7½-cup ring mold and level the surface. Bake in a 350°F oven for about 40 minutes or until well risen, golden and firm to the touch. Leave to stand in the pan for about 5 minutes, then turn out onto a rack to cool.
2. When cold, slice ½ inch thick layer from the base of the cake and set aside. Return the rest of the cake to the washed ring mold and, using a grapefruit knife, remove the center of the cake to leave a ½ inch thick shell. (Use the cut-out cake for another recipe—see Gooseberry Bakewell Tart, page 66.)
3. Fit the metal chopping blade. Place the strawberries, powdered sugar and Cointreau in the processor bowl and process for about 5 seconds, to puree. Sieve to remove any seeds. Wash the processor bowl.
4. Heat the gelatin gently until dissolved, then stir into the strawberry mixture, blending well.
5. Beat the egg white until soft peaks form, then fold into the strawberry mixture with the cream.
6. Fit the grating disc and grate the chocolate to make small curls. Fold half into the strawberry mixture.
7. Spoon into the sponge cake shell and cover with the reserved bottom slice. Cover and chill overnight or for at least 6–8 hours.
8. To make the melba sauce, fit the metal chopping blade. Place the raspberries in the processor bowl and process for about 5 seconds, to puree. Sieve to remove any seeds, then gradually beat in the powdered sugar. Chill.
9. To serve, unmold the cake onto a serving plate. Dust with a little powdered sugar and sprinkle with the remaining chocolate curls. Serve with the melba sauce.

LEMON AND GINGER SALAD

2 crisp dessert apples, cored and quartered
1 pear, cored and quartered
1 cup strawberries
2 peaches, quartered
1 banana
11 oz can lychees, drained

¼ lb black grapes, halved and seeded
FOR THE SYRUP:
2 inch piece fresh root ginger
1 small lemon, halved
1 cup sugar
⅔ cup water

1. First prepare the syrup. Fit the metal chopping blade. Place the ginger in the processor bowl and process for about 5 seconds, until finely chopped. Place in a pan.
2. Fit the slicing disc and slice the lemon. Add to the pan with the sugar and water. Heat gently until the sugar has dissolved, bring to the boil, then simmer for 5 minutes. Leave to cool.
3. Meanwhile, slice the apples, pear, strawberries, peaches and banana through the disc and place in a serving dish. Add the lychees and grapes, stirring to mix.
4. Strain the syrup over the fruit salad and toss gently to mix. Serve lightly chilled, with cream if you wish.

Serves 4–6
Preparation time: 20 minutes, plus cooling time
Cooking time: About 10 minutes
Freezing: Recommended

ST CLEMENT'S BEIGNETS

Light-as-air deep-fried choux pastry pieces sprinkled with sugar and served with an orange and lemon sauce make an elegant, if somewhat indulgent, dessert.

2-egg quantity Sweet
   Choux Pastry*
superfine sugar to sprinkle
FOR THE SAUCE:
thinly pared rind of
   1/2 lemon
thinly pared rind of
   1/4 orange

1/3 cup sugar
1 teaspoon cornstarch
1 1/4 cups water
2 tablespoons butter
1 tablespoon lemon juice
3 tablespoons orange juice

Serves 4
Preparation time: 20 minutes, plus making pastry
Cooking time: About 15 minutes
Freezing: Not recommended

1. First prepare the sauce. Fit the metal chopping blade. Place the lemon and orange rinds in the processor bowl and process for 5–8 seconds, until finely chopped.
2. Mix the sugar with the cornstarch in a pan. Gradually add the water, blending well, bring to the boil, stirring, and cook until clear and thickened. Stir in the butter, lemon and orange rind and juice. Simmer for 5 minutes. Keep warm.
3. Place the choux pastry in a piping bag fitted with a fluted tip and carefully pipe small pieces into hot oil in a deep pan. Deep-fry for 3–5 minutes, until golden.
4. Drain on paper towels and sprinkle with superfine sugar. Serve immediately, with the sauce.

GOOSEBERRY HONEY CHARLOTTE

A sumptuous summer dessert—special enough to present at a dinner party or buffet.

1/2 lb gooseberries
1–2 tablespoons orange
   juice
1 envelope gelatin, soaked
   in 3 tablespoons water
1 1/4 cups milk
3 egg yolks
1/4 cup honey

1 teaspoon lemon juice
about 16 ladies' fingers
3 tablespoons sweet sherry
2/3 cup heavy cream
1 egg white
whipped cream to decorate
   (optional)

1. Cook the gooseberries gently in the orange juice for about 10 minutes, or until tender.

2. Fit the metal chopping blade. Place the gooseberries and their liquid in the processor bowl and process for 5–6 seconds, until smooth. Remove and set aside.

3. Heat the gelatin gently until dissolved.

4. Heat the milk to just below boiling point. Beat the egg yolks and honey together, then stir into the milk. Cook gently, stirring constantly, until the custard coats the back of the spoon. Stir in the gelatin, gooseberry puree and lemon juice. Strain into a bowl and chill until on the point of setting.

5. Briefly dip the ladies' fingers in the sherry and use to line the side of a 5 cup charlotte or fluted fancy mold.

6. Whip the cream until soft peaks form (using the processor whipping blade if your model has one). Fold into the gooseberry mixture with a metal spoon.

7. Beat the egg white until stiff peaks form, then fold into the gooseberry mixture. Spoon into the lined mold and chill until set.

8. To serve, dip briefly into hot water, and carefully unmold the charlotte onto a serving plate. Decorate with swirls of whipped cream, if you wish.

Serves 6–8
Preparation time: 30 minutes, plus chilling
Cooking time: 20 minutes
Freezing: Recommended

TROPICAL CHRISTMAS CAKE

This exotic ring-shaped Christmas cake—laden with dried fruits, nuts and pineapple—has a coconut and pineapple frosting. Finish with a colorful ribbon if you wish.

8 oz can pineapple slices in
    natural juice, drained
    and juice reserved
3/4 cup butter
1/2 cup superfine sugar
2 extra large eggs
2 cups self-rising flour
1/3 cup quartered glacé
    cherries
1/2 cup chopped mixed peel

1 cup golden raisins
1/3 cup flaked coconut
1 oz angelica, chopped
1/4 cup walnut pieces
FOR THE FROSTING:
3 tablespoons butter
1 1/2 cups powdered sugar
1/3 cup flaked coconut
TO DECORATE:
glacé fruits and angelica

Makes one 6 1/4 cup ring cake
Preparation time: 30–40 minutes
Cooking time: About 1 hour
Freezing: Not recommended

1. Fit the metal chopping blade. Place the pineapple in the processor bowl and process for 2–3 seconds, until finely chopped. Remove and set aside.

2. Place the butter, sugar, eggs, flour and 3 tablespoons of the reserved pineapple juice in the processor bowl and process for about 20 seconds, until well blended.

3. Transfer to a mixing bowl and fold in the pineapple, cherries, peel, golden raisins, coconut, angelica and walnut pieces; it is better to do this by hand as most processors cannot cope with such a large quantity, but if you have a catering-size processor, process for 3–4 seconds.

4. Spoon into a greased 6 1/2 cup ring mold and bake in a 325°F oven for about 1 hour, until a skewer pierced through the center of the cake comes out clean. Leave to cool in the pan for 15 minutes, then transfer to a rack.

5. To make the frosting, melt the butter in a pan. Stir in the powdered sugar, coconut and 1 tablespoon of the reserved pineapple juice. Spread quickly over the cake and decorate with glacé fruits and angelica as you wish.

SPICED APPLE CAKE

This moist, spiced apple cake is delicious served cold, dusted with powdered sugar. It can also be served as a warm dessert with whipped cream.

1 lb cooking apples, peeled and cored
2 cups self-rising flour
1/2 teaspoon ground cloves
1/4 teaspoon grated nutmeg
2/3 cup spreadable margarine

1 cup superfine sugar
2 eggs
1/4 cup walnut pieces
sifted powdered sugar to dust

Makes one 8 inch round cake
Preparation time:
15–20 minutes
Cooking time:
1 1/2 hours
Freezing:
Not recommended

1. Grease and line a deep 8 inch round cake pan.
2. Fit the slicing disc and slice the apples. Remove and set aside. Wash the processor bowl.
3. Fit the metal chopping blade. Place the flour, cloves and nutmeg in the processor bowl and process for about 1 second, to sift. Add the margarine, sugar and eggs and process for 10–12 seconds, until well blended. Add the walnuts and process for 1–2 seconds, to mix.
4. Spoon half of the cake mixture into the prepared pan and spread evenly. Cover with the apple slices, then top with the remaining cake mixture; do not worry too much about spreading evenly, as the mixture will cover the apples during cooking.
5. Bake in a 325°F oven for about 1 1/2 hours, until well risen, golden and a skewer pierced through the center of the cake comes out clean. Leave to cool in the pan if serving cold.
6. Transfer to a serving plate and dust with powdered sugar.

GINGERBREAD SLICES

This delicious moist gingerbread is best allowed to mature for a few days before eating.

4 cups all-purpose flour
3 teaspoons ground ginger
3 teaspoons baking powder
1 teaspoon baking soda
1 teaspoon salt
1 cup light brown granulated sugar

3/4 cup sweet butter
1/2 cup molasses
3/4 cup golden syrup, or 1/2 light corn syrup and 1/2 molasses
1 1/4 cups milk
1 egg, beaten

1. Grease and line a deep 9 inch square cake pan.
2. Fit the metal chopping or plastic blending blade. Place the flour, ginger, baking powder, baking soda and salt in the processor bowl and process for about 3 seconds, to sift.
3. Place the sugar, butter, molasses and syrup in a pan and heat gently until melted.
4. With the motor running, pour the butter mixture, milk and egg through the feed tube and process for 8–10 seconds, until well blended.
5. Pour into the prepared pan and bake in a 350°F oven for about 1½ hours or until well risen and just firm to the touch.
6. Leave to cool in the pan for 15 minutes, then turn out onto a rack. When completely cold, wrap in foil, without removing the waxed paper, and store for 4–7 days to mature. Cut into slices to serve.

Makes one 9 inch square cake
Preparation time: 15 minutes
Cooking time: 1½ hours
Freezing: Recommended

HONEY CARROT CAKE

4 large carrots
2 cups all-purpose flour
½ teaspoon salt
¾ teaspoon baking soda
1 teaspoon baking powder
½ teaspoon ground
   cinnamon
½ cup sugar
3 tablespoons honey
2 eggs, beaten
⅓ cup salad oil

14 oz can crushed
   pineapple, drained
¼ cup walnut pieces
FOR THE FROSTING:
1 cup powdered sugar
3 tablespoons butter
3 tablespoons cream cheese
½ teaspoon vanilla
1–2 teaspoons milk
TO DECORATE:
walnut halves

Makes one 7 inch round cake
Preparation time: 20 minutes
Cooking time: 35–40 minutes
Freezing: Not recommended

1. Grease and line a deep 7 inch round cake pan.
2. Fit the grating disc and grate the carrots. Set aside.
3. Fit the metal chopping blade. Place the flour, salt, baking soda, baking powder, cinnamon and sugar in the processor bowl and process for 3–4 seconds, to sift.
4. Add the honey, eggs, oil, pineapple, walnuts and grated carrot and process for 8–10 seconds, to mix.
5. Pour into the prepared pan and bake in a 350°F oven for 35–40 minutes. Cool on a rack.
6. To make the frosting, place the ingredients in the processor bowl and process for 10 seconds, until smooth.
7. Spread and swirl over the top and side of the cake. Decorate with walnut halves to serve.

FILBERT AND BANANA TEA LOAF

The addition of bananas gives this a good moist texture and excellent keeping quality. Serve plain or buttered.

⅓ cup filberts
2 bananas
½ cup butter
¾ cup dark brown sugar,
   packed

2 eggs
2 cups self-rising flour
1 teaspoon baking powder
2 tablespoons milk

1. Grease and line a 6½ × 3¾ × 3 inch loaf pan.
2. Fit the metal chopping blade. Place the filberts in the processor bowl and process for about 3 seconds, until coarsely chopped. Remove and set aside.
3. Place the bananas in the processor bowl and process for about 4 seconds, until smooth. Remove and set aside. Wash the processor bowl.

4. Place the butter, sugar, eggs, flour, baking powder and milk in the processor bowl and process for about 10 seconds, until well blended. Add the bananas and filberts and process for 1–2 seconds, to mix.

5. Spoon into the prepared pan and level the surface. Bake in a 350°F oven for about 1 hour or until the loaf is well risen, golden brown and firm to the touch. Turn out onto a rack to cool.

Makes one loaf
Preparation time:
15 minutes
Cooking time:
1 hour
Freezing:
Recommended

ORANGE AND ALMOND LOAF

A rich fruit and nut loaf that will keep in an airtight
container for 2–3 weeks.

3 cups raisins
2/3 cup tropical fruit juice
2/3 cup blanched almonds
3 cups self-rising flour

1/4 cup butter
2 oranges
1/4 cup superfine sugar
3 tablespoons milk
2 eggs

Makes one loaf
Preparation time:
20 minutes
Cooking time:
About 1 hour
Freezing:
Recommended

1. Fit the metal chopping blade. Place the raisins in the
processor bowl and process for 2–4 seconds, until coarsely chopped. Place in a pan with the tropical fruit juice,
bring slowly to the boil, then remove from the heat and set
aside.
2. Place the almonds in the processor bowl and process
for about 2 seconds, until coarsely chopped. Remove and
set aside.
3. Place the flour and butter in the processor bowl and
process for 7–8 seconds, until the mixture resembles fine
breadcrumbs.
4. Finely grate the orange rinds, discard the pith and chop
the flesh.
5. Add the sugar, almonds, raisin mixture, milk, eggs and
orange rind to the processor bowl and process for 8–10
seconds, until well blended. Add the orange flesh and
process for 1–2 seconds, to mix.
6. Pour into a greased 6½ × 3¾ × 3 inch loaf pan and
bake in a 350°F oven for about 1 hour. Cool on a rack and
cut into thin slices to serve.

HARVEST VICTORIA CAKE

A Victoria sponge cake with a delicious difference—the
top is baked with a colorful fruit and nut topping.

grated rind of 2 lemons
2-egg quantity Victoria
    Sandwich Cake Mixture*
1 oz colored glacé cherries,
    quartered
1 tablespoon chopped
    mixed peel

2 tablespoons slivered
    almonds
FOR THE BUTTER CREAM:
1 cup sifted powdered
    sugar
1/4 cup butter
1 tablespoon lemon juice

1. Grease two 7 inch round cake pans and line the bases.
2. Add the lemon rind to the prepared cake mixture in the processor bowl and process for 1–2 seconds, to mix.
3. Divide the mixture between the prepared pans and smooth the tops. Sprinkle one cake evenly with the glacé cherries, peel and almonds.
4. Bake in a 350°F oven for 25–30 minutes or until the tops spring back when lightly pressed. Leave to cool in the pans for 2–3 minutes, then transfer to a rack.
5. Meanwhile, wash the processor bowl and fit the metal chopping or plastic blending blade. Place the powdered sugar, butter and lemon juice in the processor bowl and process for about 5 seconds, until smooth.
6. To serve, sandwich the cakes together with the lemon butter cream, placing the fruit-topped cake on top.

Makes one 7 inch cake
Preparation time: 10–15 minutes, plus making cake mixture
Cooking time: 25–30 minutes
Freezing: Recommended

GOOSEBERRY BAKEWELL TART

This is a scrumptious tart to make when you have a little left-over plain cake. Once cut, the rich, crisp and golden topping reveals the gooey jam filling.

8 oz Basic Pastry*
3 tablespoons gooseberry jam
FOR THE TOPPING:
3 oz pound cake or other plain cake
¼ cup butter

¼ cup superfine sugar
grated rind of ½ lemon
1 extra large egg
¾ cup ground almonds
1 tablespoon lemon juice or milk
powdered sugar to dust

Serves 6
Preparation time:
25 minutes, plus making pastry
Cooking time:
30–40 minutes
Freezing:
Recommended

1. Roll out the pastry on a lightly floured surface and use to line an 8 inch deep pie plate. Trim and flute the edges of the tart.
2. Spread the jam evenly over the pastry base.
3. To make the topping, fit the metal chopping blade, place the cake in the processor bowl and process for about 3 seconds, to make fine crumbs. Add the butter, sugar, lemon rind, egg, almonds and lemon juice or milk and process for 10–12 seconds, until well blended.
4. Spread the topping evenly over the gooseberry jam and smooth the surface.
5. Bake in a 400°F oven, for 30–40 minutes or until well risen, golden and firm to the touch.
6. Serve warm or cold, dusted with a little powdered sugar.

FRUIT AND CINNAMON SCONES

Healthy and wholesome, fruit and cinnamon scones can be made with almost any combination of dried fruits, including apricots, raisins and those suggested here. The quantities below give excellent results.

½ oz dried bananas
½ oz dried pears
½ oz dried apples
½ oz dried figs
2 cups whole wheat flour
pinch of salt
1 tablespoon baking powder

½ teaspoon ground cinnamon
¼ cup butter
2 tablespoons superfine sugar
⅔ cup milk
milk to glaze

1. Fit the metal chopping blade. Place the bananas, pears, apples and figs in the processor bowl and process for 3–5 seconds, until coarsely chopped. Remove and set aside.

2. Place the flour, salt, baking powder, cinnamon and butter in the processor bowl and process for about 5 seconds, until the mixture resembles fine breadcrumbs.

3. Add the sugar and dried fruit. With the motor running, add the milk through the feed tube and process for 4–6 seconds, to make a soft dough. Turn onto a lightly floured surface and knead until smooth.

4. Roll out to about ½ inch thickness and cut out 12 circles using a 2 inch cutter. Place on a greased baking sheet and brush with milk.

5. Bake in a 425°F oven for 8–10 minutes or until well risen and golden. Cool on a rack.

Makes 12
Preparation time: 10–15 minutes
Cooking time: 8–10 minutes
Freezing: Recommended

FARMHOUSE FESTIVAL LOAF

Home-made bread can become an everyday luxury, especially if you mix and knead the dough in the processor, then leave it to prove overnight in the refrigerator ready for baking the following morning.

½ oz fresh yeast
½ teaspoon molasses
1 cup warm water
3 cups whole wheat flour
½ teaspoon salt

1½ teaspoons sunflower
*   oil*
buckwheat, bulgur wheat,
*   seeds or nuts to sprinkle*
*   (optional)*

Makes one loaf
Preparation time:
30 minutes, plus rising time
Cooking time:
15–30 minutes
Freezing:
Recommended

1. Cream the yeast and molasses with a third of the water. Leave in a warm place for about 5 minutes, until frothy.
2. Fit the metal chopping blade. Place the flour, salt and oil in the processor bowl. With the motor running, add the yeast liquid and remaining water through the feed tube; process for 30 seconds, to blend and knead the dough.
3. Cover the processor bowl with plastic wrap and leave to rise in a warm place for 1½–2 hours, until doubled in size.
4. Process for about 10–15 seconds, to knock back and knead the dough.
5. Flatten the dough out to a rectangle about 1 inch thick. Fold into three, like an envelope, and tuck the 2 short ends over the seam to fit the pan. Place seam-side down in a greased 7½ × 3½ × 2½ inch loaf pan.
6. Cover with plastic wrap and leave to rise in a warm place for 30 minutes to 1 hour, until almost doubled in size. Sprinkle with buckwheat, bulgur wheat, seeds or nuts, or a combination, if you wish.
7. Bake in a 425°F oven for 25–30 minutes, until the bread sounds hollow when tapped underneath. Turn out and cool on a rack.

VARIATIONS
Braid: Divide the dough into 3 equal pieces. Roll each into a long strand and braid them loosely together, starting in the center and working to each end in turn. Dampen the ends and pinch together to seal. Place on a greased baking sheet and proceed as above.

Cloverleaf Rolls: Divide the dough into 6 equal portions, then divide each into 3 pieces. Shape each piece into a small ball. Place in groups of 3 on a greased baking sheet and proceed as above, cooking for 15–20 minutes.

BEAN BURGERS

½ lb lean beef
½ teaspoon French
  mustard
1 tablespoon chopped
  parsley
8 oz can baked beans
salt and pepper to taste
oil for brushing

TO SERVE:
4 small whole wheat buns,
  halved and lightly
  toasted
4 lettuce leaves
2 tomatoes, sliced
tomato catsup (optional)

Serves 4
Preparation time:
15 minutes, plus
chilling
Cooking time:
10 minutes
Freezing:
Recommended at
end of stage 2, if
fresh meat used

1. Fit the metal chopping blade. Place the beef in the processor bowl and process for 5–6 seconds, to grind. Add the mustard, parsley, beans, and salt and pepper, and process for 2–3 seconds, to mix.
2. Divide and shape into 4 burgers and chill for 1 hour.
3. Brush with oil and broil for 5 minutes on each side. Serve in a bun, with lettuce, tomato, and catsup if you wish.

ALL SEASONS MEATLOAF

8 slices whole wheat bread,
  cubed
1 onion
1 lb chuck or braising steak
½ lb diced casserole pork

2 oz mushrooms
1 tablespoon tomato paste
1 egg
⅔ cup vegetable stock or
  tomato juice

Serves 8
Preparation time:
15 minutes
Cooking time:
About 1½ hours
Freezing:
Recommended

1. Fit the metal chopping blade. With the motor running, add the bread cubes through the feed tube and process to make crumbs. Remove and set aside.
2. Place the onion in the processor bowl and process for 4–5 seconds, until finely chopped. Remove and set aside.
3. Place the steak and pork in the processor bowl and process for 8–10 seconds, to grind. Add all the remaining ingredients and process for 5–7 seconds, until well mixed.
4. Spoon into a greased 6½ × 3¾ × 3 inch loaf pan, press down firmly and cover with foil. Bake in a 350°F oven for about 1½ hours, until firm.
5. Turn out and slice, then serve with vegetables or salad.

COTTAGE ONE-POTS

An ideal dinner for older babies and toddlers—well worth keeping a supply in the freezer.

1 strip bacon	8 oz can tomatoes,
1 onion	chopped
1 celery stick	1/4 cup meat or vegetable
1 large carrot	stock
1 lb braising lamb	1 lb potatoes, boiled
1 tablespoon salad oil	1/2 cup cottage cheese
	1–2 tablespoons milk

Serves 6–8
Preparation time:
25–30 minutes
Cooking time:
15–20 minutes
Freezing:
Recommended for
up to 3 months

1. Fit the metal chopping blade. Place the bacon in the processor bowl and process for 2–3 seconds, to chop.
2. Add the onion, celery and carrot and process for about 5 seconds, to chop. Remove and set aside.
3. Place the lamb in the processor bowl and process for 8–10 seconds, to grind. Remove and set aside. Wash the processor bowl.
4. Heat the oil in a pan, add the bacon and vegetable mixture and fry for 5 minutes. Add the lamb and cook for about 10 minutes, until lightly browned.
5. Stir in the tomatoes with their juice and the stock. Simmer for about 15 minutes, until thickened. Divide between 6–8 ramekins or small ovenproof dishes.
6. Fit the metal chopping blade. Place the potatoes, cottage cheese and milk in the processor bowl and process for 4–6 seconds, until a smooth puree forms; time carefully, making sure not to over-process. Spoon or pipe attractively over the lamb mixture.
7. Bake in a 400°F oven for 15–20 minutes, until golden.

NUT AND OAT SLICES

1/2 cup butter	1/2 cup rolled oats
1/2 cup dark brown sugar,	3 tablespoons natural bran
packed	1/2 cup walnut pieces
2 eggs	FOR THE FROSTING:
2 tablespoons milk	1/2 cup cream cheese
3/4 cup all-purpose flour	2 teaspoons powdered
2 teaspoons baking	sugar
powder	3 tablespoons orange juice

1. Grease and line a shallow 8 inch square cake pan.
2. Fit the metal chopping or plastic blending blade. Place the butter, sugar, eggs, milk, flour, baking powder, oats and bran in the processor bowl and process for 10–12 seconds, until well blended. Add the walnuts and process for 1–2 seconds, to mix.
3. Spoon into the prepared pan and spread evenly. Bake in a 375°F oven for 20–25 minutes, or until firm but springy to the touch. Leave to cool slightly in the pan, then turn out onto a rack.
4. To make the frosting, fit the metal chopping or plastic blending blade. Place all the ingredients in the cleaned processor bowl and process for about 5 seconds, until smooth.
5. Swirl the frosting over the cooled cake with a palette knife. Cut into slices to serve.

Makes 16
Preparation time:
20–25 minutes
Cooking time:
20–25 minutes
Freezing:
Not recommended

YOGURTY FRUIT DESSERTS

These desserts are perfect for lunchboxes—simply cover with plastic wrap.

1 envelope gelatin　　　　　*1¹/₄ cups raspberry yogurt*
1¹/₄ cups red grape juice　　*few raspberries to decorate*
³/₄ cup raspberries

Makes 4–6
Preparation time:
10 minutes, plus chilling
Freezing:
Not recommended

1. Sprinkle the gelatin over the grape juice and leave to soften. Heat gently in a pan until dissolved.
2. Fit the metal chopping blade. Place the grape juice, raspberries and yogurt in the processor bowl and process for about 5 seconds to blend.
3. Pour into individual dishes, pots or fancy molds and chill until set.
4. If using fancy molds, dip briefly into hot water and turn out onto small plates. Decorate with a few whole raspberries to serve.

TROPICAL FRUIT DESSERT

An exotic selection of tropical fruits pureed together to make a delicious dessert suitable for the very young, and popular with older children too. Serve one portion and freeze the remainder. As a guide, very young babies will probably eat 1 cube per serving, babies from 4–6 months may need 2 cubes, and those aged 6–9 months should be offered 3 cubes.

1 large ripe banana
¹/₃ lb melon

¹/₂ guava, mango or papaya, peeled and pitted or seeded

1. Fit the metal chopping blade. Place all the fruit in the processor bowl and process for 3–5 seconds, until smooth. Sieve to remove any seeds if necessary.
2. Serve one portion immediately. Spoon the remainder into deep ice cube trays, wrap in foil and freeze until firm. Thaw thoroughly to serve.

Makes about 30 cubes
Preparation time: 5–10 minutes
Freezing: Recommended for up to 1 month

VARIATIONS
Replace the guava, mango or papaya with 1 ripe pear; ¹/₃ cup cooked apple; 1 cup strawberries; a large peeled peach; or 2–3 peeled apricots.

COTTAGE CHEESE FRUIT SAVORY

This is a first 'solid' fruit savory for the very young—introduce at about 3–4 months. See above for serving guidelines. If you prefer, replace the mango with a large ripe papaya or 2 small bananas.

1 large mango, peeled
¹/₂ cup cottage cheese
¹/₃ cup pineapple juice

1 teaspoon honey (optional)

1. Fit the metal chopping blade. Place the mango flesh in the processor bowl and process for about 2 seconds, to chop.
2. Add the cottage cheese, pineapple juice and honey, if using, and process for 2 seconds, until smooth.
3. Serve immediately; spoon the remainder into deep ice cube trays, wrap in foil and freeze until firm. Thaw thoroughly to serve.

Makes about 20 cubes
Preparation time: 5–10 minutes
Freezing: Recommended for up to 2 months

BASIC RECIPES

BASIC BATTER

This quantity is sufficient to make one large Yorkshire pudding or toad-in-the-hole or about 8 medium-size crepes.

1 cup all-purpose flour   *1 tablespoon salad oil*
pinch of salt   *1¼ cups milk, or milk and*
1 egg   *water mixed*

**Makes about
1¼ cups
Preparation time:**
5 minutes
Freezing:
Not recommended

1. Fit the metal chopping or plastic blending blade. Place the flour, salt, egg, oil and half of the liquid in the processor bowl and process for about 15 seconds, to mix.
2. Add the remaining liquid and process for 15 seconds. Use as required.

CHOUX PASTRY

Choux pastry is perhaps one of the most intriguing pastries because it hardly looks like a pastry at all until cooked. Simple to make, it is used for éclairs, gougeres, profiteroles and sweet or savory filled puffs. This quantity makes sufficient for 25–30 profiteroles, 10 éclairs, 1 puff ring or gougere or 10 small puffs.

⅔ cup all-purpose flour   *⅔ cup water*
pinch of salt   *2 eggs*
¼ cup butter, diced

**Makes a 2-egg
quantity
Preparation time:**
10–15 minutes
Freezing:
Recommended;
shape and freeze
before baking

1. Fit the metal chopping blade. Place the flour and salt in the processor bowl and process for about 1 second, to sift.
2. Place the butter and water in a pan, heat slowly to melt the butter, then bring to a fast boil.
3. With the motor running, quickly add to the processor bowl through the feed tube and process for about 3 seconds, to blend.
4. Add the eggs, one at a time, and process until thick and glossy. Use as required.

VARIATION
Sweet Choux Pastry: Prepare as above, adding 1 teaspoon superfine sugar to the water and butter mixture.

BASIC PASTRY

A quick and easy one-stage pastry suitable for pies and tarts. This quantity is sufficient for an 8 inch tart, 12 double-crust tartlets or 1 large pie crust.

2 cups all-purpose flour
¼ teaspoon salt
¼ cup butter, diced

⅓ cup vegetable
shortening, diced
2 tablespoons ice water

1. Fit the metal chopping blade. Place the flour, salt, butter and shortening in the processor bowl and process for 7–8 seconds, until the mixture resembles fine breadcrumbs.
2. With the motor running, add the water slowly through the feed tube and process until the ingredients just bind together to make a ball.
3. Turn onto a lightly floured surface and knead until smooth. Wrap in foil or plastic wrap and chill for 15 minutes before using.

Makes ½ lb
Preparation time: 5 minutes, plus chilling
Freezing: Recommended

VARIATIONS

Whole Wheat Basic Pastry: Use whole wheat flour instead of all-purpose flour and 2–3 tablespoons ice water.

Cheese Basic Pastry: Fit the grating disc and grate 3 oz Cheddar cheese. Remove and set aside. Fit the metal chopping blade. Prepare as above, but add ½ teaspoon dry mustard with the flour, and the grated cheese with the water.

Rich Sweet Basic Pastry: Fit the metal chopping blade. Place 1½ cups all-purpose flour, ⅓ cup diced butter and 2 tablespoons superfine sugar in the processor bowl and process as above. With the motor running, add 1 egg yolk and 1 tablespoon ice water through the feed tube and process as above.

Nut Basic Pastry: Prepare as above, adding ¼ cup chopped nuts with the ice water.

Herby Basic Pastry: Prepare as above, adding 1½–2 teaspoons dried herbs with the flour.

Lemon Basic Pastry: Prepare as above, adding the grated rind of ½ lemon with the flour.

HOT WATER CRUST PASTRY

A crisp rich pastry used to make meat pies and picnic or buffet table fare. This quantity is sufficient for a loaf-shaped pie, a 6 inch round pie or 4 individual double-crust pies.

3 cups all-purpose flour
1 teaspoon salt
⅔ cup shortening, diced

⅔ cup water, or milk and
water mixed

Makes ¾ lb
Preparation time:
10–15 minutes
Freezing:
Not recommended

1. Fit the metal chopping blade. Place the flour and salt in the processor bowl and process for about 1 second, to sift.
2. Place the shortening and liquid in a pan, heat slowly to melt the shortening, then bring to a fast boil.
3. With the motor running, quickly add to the processor bowl through the feed tube and process for about 3 seconds, to blend.
4. Turn onto a lightly floured surface and knead until smooth. Use as required, while still warm.

VARIATION

Whole Wheat Hot Water Crust Pastry: Use whole wheat flour instead of all-purpose and increase the liquid to 1 cup.

WHIPPED DANISH CREAM

A useful cream made with butter, milk and gelatin. It produces a cream with a thick pouring consistency which can be whipped lightly to form soft peaks.

½ cup sweet butter, diced
⅔ cup milk
½ teaspoon gelatin,
soaked in 2 teaspoons
cold water

1–2 teaspoons superfine
sugar (optional)

Makes 1¼ cups
Preparation time:
10–15 minutes,
plus chilling
Freezing:
Not recommended

1. Place the butter and milk in a pan and heat gently until melted; do not allow to boil.
2. Add a little of the milk to the gelatin and stir well. Return to the pan with the sugar, if using, blending well.
3. Fit the metal chopping, plastic blending or whipping blade. Pour the cream mixture into the processor bowl and process for 30 seconds. Pour into a bowl and chill for 3–4 hours or overnight. Use as required.

VICTORIA SANDWICH CAKE MIXTURE

Light, spongy and endlessly versatile, this one-stage Victoria sandwich cake mixture will prove invaluable for making small cakes, large elaborate gateaux and speedy sponge-topped fruit puddings. This quantity is sufficient for a 7 inch cake.

1 cup self-rising flour
3/4 teaspoon baking
*   powder*

1/2 cup spreadable
*   margarine*
1/2 cup superfine sugar
2 eggs

Makes a 2-egg quantity
Preparation time:
10–15 minutes
Freezing:
Recommended when baked

Fit the metal chopping or plastic blending blade. Place all the ingredients in the processor bowl and process for 10–12 seconds, until well blended. Use as required.

MAYONNAISE

3 egg yolks
1/2 teaspoon salt
1/2 teaspoon dry mustard
pinch of ground red pepper

5 teaspoons white wine
*   vinegar or lemon juice*
1 1/4 cups olive or other
*   salad oil*

Makes about 1 1/4 cups
Preparation time:
5 minutes
Freezing:
Not recommended

1. Fit the metal chopping blade. Place the egg yolks, salt, dry mustard, ground red pepper and 3 teaspoons of the vinegar or lemon juice in the processor bowl and process for about 3 seconds, to blend.
2. With the motor running, add the oil in a steady stream through the feed tube and process until thick and glossy.
3. Add the remaining vinegar or lemon juice and process for about 1 second, to blend. Use as required.

VARIATIONS
Use tarragon, cider or herb vinegar for a change.

Garlic Mayonnaise: Prepare as above, adding 1/2–1 teaspoon garlic puree (see page 6) with the final vinegar.

Green or Herb Mayonnaise: Fit the metal chopping blade. Place 2 scallions, 3 parsley sprigs, 1 tarragon sprig and a few chives in the processor bowl and process until finely chopped. Remove and set aside. Prepare the mayonnaise as above, adding the herbs with the final vinegar.

INDEX

Photography by: Martin Brigdale
Designed by: Sue Storey
Home economist: Lyn Rutherford
Stylist: Alison Williams
Illustration by: Linda Smith
U.S. Consultant Editor: Carla Capalbo